CONTENTS

Chapter 1: Changing Your Mindset Towards Investing   3
Chapter 2: Anyone Can Learn to Become a Successful Investor   6
Chapter 3: Invest In What You Know   9
Chapter 4: Suitability   12
Chapter 5: Dividends   18
Chapter 6: Moats Matter   27
Chapter 7: Value Investing   29
Chapter 8: Diversification   40
Chapter 9: Risk vs Reward   45
Chapter 10: Mutual Funds   50
Chapter 11: Seeking and Paying for Investment Advice   52

Prologue

I wanted to write this book about investing in stocks because I believe that deeply ingrained in all of us is a desire to contribute to society in one form or another. We now live in a society with ever-increasing change, and while that change has opened up an unprecedented amount career mobility and opportunity, it also ushers in a greater level of uncertainty and a feeling of a lack of control over our livelihoods. This book is designed to help you take back control over your livelihood by teaching you the art and science of investing through a generosity-minded approach.

Having a generosity-minded investment attitude means investing in stocks of everyday companies that you can well-understand their role and benefit to society, with the goal of building an extra growing stream of income that you can rely on in both good times and bad. What this book will not teach is trading strategies that aim to help you turn a quick profit, which I believe to be not only time-consuming but also unsustainable for most people. Instead, what I advocate for and will teach is a buy-and-hold, value-minded approach towards investing in dividend-paying companies that you can understand. I truly believe that with the proper education and a mindset towards looking for value, investing creates a sense of meaning, purpose, and engagement in your life that can lead to long-term wealth and happiness.

CHAPTER 1: CHANGING YOUR MINDSET TOWARDS INVESTING

Think back to human history, to the agrarian age in which our ancestors lived in small communities and everyone had a specific role to play. Societies back then were every bit as dynamic as they are today, but they just operated on a much smaller scale. Today, most of us work in companies where we hopefully have the same sense of community and pride in what we do. However, the work environment of today is very different from that of generations past. Gone are the days when you can expect to work at a company for your entire career and collect a comfortable pension in retirement. There is far more uncertainty in today's work environment. There are many things that you can control, such as your work ethic and sharpening of your skills, yet there are far more things that are beyond your control.

For many people, a natural response to this level of uncertainty is to amass more money in your bank account to ease anxiety and guard against uncertainty. After all, who does not want a big bank account? But let's go extreme and say that you've just won the $1 Billion Powerball jackpot, which is more money than anyone can reasonably spend in a lifetime. However, say it comes with the catch that you can only use the money for the direct benefit of you and your family, whether it be the acquisition of a luxurious home, cars, yachts, and exquisite vacations. While that may sound enticing at first, I can assure you that you will be tired of this lifestyle after 3 months and the reason why is because your life would be devoid of meaning and purpose.

A cure for this void is to re-engage yourself with society by investing a portion of your newly found wealth into income producing assets, whether it be stocks, bonds, or real estate. Some may call that selfish, because after all, why would you need to grow your money after you have all the money in the world? But I would say investing is the opposite of being selfish. By investing in a company such as Microsoft, you are providing valuable technology to businesses that employ millions of people around the world. Or through investment in an REIT such as Federal Realty Trust, you are providing valuable infrastructure to grocery stores and restaurants that serve many small business owners, their employees, and customers. And by purchasing those assets, you are freeing up precious capital that the seller of those shares can use to invest in other businesses, such as a new startup that aims to fulfill an unmet need.

I truly believe that when well-researched and with a well-balanced understanding of risk versus reward, investing is an honorable action because while the investor expects to receive a profit, he is in effect bearing risk and spurring economic growth for that profit. One could take a low risk approach by just keeping all of one's money in a savings account, but that would essentially be bearing zero risk for a very low rate of return. Don't get me wrong, savings accounts provide an essential safety net to fulfill everyday living expenses and every household should have at least 9 months-worth of basic living expenses in savings. But I would argue that having all of your money in a savings account is actually riskier than investing a portion of that money, because your purchasing power would be steadily eroded over time by the constant march of inflation.

One may think that to become wealthy through investing

is an all-to-daunting task, and that a great investor such as Warren Buffett is a once in a lifetime superstar. But for every great household name such as Buffett, there are countless everyday people who became great disciplined investors that the general public never heard about. Take Grace Groner for example. Grace was born in 1909 with humble beginnings. She took her first job as a secretary with Abbott Laboratories and purchased three $60 shares in her employer for a total of $180. After many stock splits and continued dividend reinvestment, her stake in Abbott was worth $7 Million by the time she passed away in 2010. She bequeathed her fortune to her alma mater, Lake Forest College, whose administrators were pleasantly surprised along with her friends to learn that she had amassed such a fortune.

Of course, I would never advise anyone to put all of their eggs in one basket as Grace did with Abbott Labs. Grace was very fortunate to have worked for an immensely successful company that rewarded its shareholders so well. But what this inspiring story does speak to is 1.) The power of compounding and how it can work wonders for an investment portfolio and 2.) Achieving wealth through stock market investing is more common than you think, but it takes discipline and the right mindset to achieve it.

I'd like to close this chapter by saying that wealth is more of a mindset than an actual dollar figure. Attaining wealth is a journey rather than an end state. By making a habit of good investment practices and adopting the mindset of living below your means, wealth can be attained over time through the power of compounding returns.

CHAPTER 2: ANYONE CAN LEARN TO BECOME A SUCCESSFUL INVESTOR

Anyone can learn to become a successful investor. Note that I said learn, because no matter how smart you are, investing does not come innate to anyone. It has to be learned just like any other important life skill. Since the first day of school until the glorious day of graduation, we are taught to hone in on a specific set of skills that can make us marketable for employment. There is nothing inherently wrong with this model, as it is necessary for the proper function and advancement of society. The educational system is designed to continuously train and deliver a professional workforce that can effectively carry on the torch from the prior generation as they age and retire. This is an honorable and effective model that has served our society well and has effectively been the pathway for many to afford a comfortable living and build a family.

However, what is inherent in this model is the narrow focus in which the participant solely focuses on the mentality "what skills can I trade to an employer to afford my house, car, lifestyle, and a comfortable retirement?" And if you focus only on this narrow-minded mentality, you will never be truly wealthy because at the end of the day, there is only so much that you can contribute to society from an individual standpoint. Of course, there are examples of those at the top of their fields who have gone on to win Nobel prizes for groundbreaking work in their respective fields. But let's be real here. While you should aspire for greatness in your field of expertise and do your very best work at all times, chances are that you're not going to win a Nobel Prize nor become the next CEO of your company. There are simply not enough spots at the top of the professional pyramid.

In today's dynamic work environment, it is important to not only constantly update and sharpen your skills as an employee, but to also expand beyond the narrow-focused mindset of trading tit for tat into what I call a generosity mindset of employing your earned capital for the betterment of society through investing. A great amount of wealth lies beyond just working for a paycheck in a narrow-focused mindset to having your money work hard for you. As a famous investor once said: "You'll never become wealthy until you figure out a way to make money while you sleep."

What role does having a generosity-mindset and investing have in common, you might ask? The answer is a lot! By investing in a company say, Walgreens, you are providing millions of people, including your own family, friends, and neighbors with a convenient and easily accessible way to obtain their medications and the dividends and capital gains that you receive in return are the reciprocity for you providing that service. While you are unlikely to accumulate a significant stake in a company like Walgreens such that warrants the attention of the Board of Directors, you can take comfort in knowing that Walgreens cannot exist without investors such as yourself, and that the more you believe in the company through the accumulation of shares, the more the company will reward & enrich you through dividends and capital gains in return.

James Ma

Getting Educated about Stocks

I've often heard people say that the stock market is like a casino and that stocks are risky. I would say that stocks are indeed risky for those who do not properly educate themselves about investing. To draw an analogy, downhill skiing appears to be risky for the untrained skier, but for a trained and experienced skier, it is not risky. The majority of people have never had any investment education because the K-12 educational system is designed to prepare you for the workforce rather than prepare you to be an investor.

An uninformed investor may approach the market as if it were a casino, and if you treat it as such, the market will eat up your principal as if it were a casino. This includes acting on a hot stock tip or chasing a momentum stock without first doing the proper research on your own. To become an informed investor, one must have the motivation to read and learn about prudent investing methods and do proper research on the stocks before making a purchase. In the following chapters, you will learn how to properly value stocks and to develop an investment methodology. You will also learn to embrace stock price volatility so that you can acquire stocks at value prices. Learning about investing takes time, effort, and motivation, just like any other subject that you want to master.

CHAPTER 3: INVEST IN WHAT YOU KNOW

Investing in what you know is key to having a generosity-mindset. After all, how can you feel good about the service that your investment is providing if you don't really understand what the company does? You may not have realized it yet, but many of the best investment opportunities that you can make are right under your nose. For example, I know a person that buys a lot of goods from Costco for his business. He understands the Costco business model better than anyone and he probably ranks in the Top 5% of all Costco customers. Imagine if he had also participated in Costco's impressive growth story by purchasing shares. He would have enjoyed both the capital appreciation in the stock price as well as the quarterly dividends being increased every year.

Costco has done incredibly well in spite of intense competition from both brick and mortar players such as Target and Walmart as well as e-commerce behemoth Amazon. They have learned not only to adapt but have also thrived in an omni-channel environment by building upon both their physical and online presence with the physical and online components often complementing each other. By giving their online customers the option to pick up in store, traditional retailers that have successfully shifted to this omni-channel strategy have found that these customers tend to buy additional items in-store upon pick up, thereby increasing foot traffic and sales. Effective management such as that of Costco not only acknowledges change, but also adapts to and in some cases, lead change in their respective industries.

Surely my friend who is a loyal customer of Costco could have easily picked up on Costco's successful business model, and had he decided to participate in Costco strategy by purchasing shares, he would have enjoyed the impressive capital appreciation in the shares over the years, and not to mention the increasing quarterly dividend payments that would be the icing on the cake. Another example would be that if you worked in the telecom industry, you would probably understand the ever-increasing role of fiber in enabling the next generation of communications technology. We are living in an ever-increasingly connected world dubbed the Internet of Things (IoT), where billions of every day devices from cars to thermostats can communicate with one another. One such company that is riding this wave is Corning, a leading manufacturer of fiber optics that is the backbone of 5G technology and the internet of things. Corning investors have done well over the years for riding the wave of an inter-connected world.

You don't have to be an expert in a field to invest in that field. Today, we are living in a world with an unprecedented wealth of publicly available information and research that was once hard to attain and/or reserved for big money Wall Street professionals. For example, there are online investment communities such as Seeking Alpha, subscription services such as Forbes newsletters, and investment analyst reports such as Morningstar where you can learn about leading companies and industries. For beginner investors who may not fully understand some of the financial jargon being tossed around, I recommend looking them up on Investopedia.com, which is an easy-to-understand online encyclopedia for financial terms and metrics. Other websites such as Yahoo Finance provide a host of current and historical financial measures and ratios that you can use to evaluate and compare different stocks. The key is having the interest to learn about investment ideas and the willingness to do your own homework, whether it be looking at the company's financials, or reading through the company's latest annual report (10-K), which is usually available on their investor relations website and on Sec.gov no cost to you.

CHAPTER 4: SUITABILITY

How many times have you seen or heard the phrase "Buying this company is like buying Amazon in 1997"? Amazon has had an incredible run since its IPO debuted in 1997. A $10,000 investment in Amazon at IPO would be worth more than $10 Million today. If you hear someone offering you an idea to turn $10,000 into $10 Million, then the first question that you should ask yourself is: "If I found a stock that could turn $10,000 into $10 Million in twenty years, then would I tell anybody about it, or keep the information to myself so that I could buy up as many shares as I can?" The answer to this question should be obvious. You should run away from that person as fast as you can.

All companies face an uncertain future, and the Amazon back in 1997 was in a far more precarious position than the Amazon of today. Back then, Amazon had virtually no moat and a much bigger competitor could have easily swooped in and taken them out. A bet in Amazon in 1997 was a risky one in Jeff Bezos (a virtual unknown back then), and that with a substantial amount of hard work, ingenuity, and luck, his vision would pan out into the immensely successful company that it is today.

The goal for successful investing should be to find a suitable investment philosophy for yourself. If you have a knack for uncovering hidden gems such as Amazon in 1997 and have the technical expertise to do so, then that could be your niche. However, you must do so with the understanding that young and unproven companies carry a lot of risk, and that you must be prepared to do your homework, have optimism, and stick with your convictions through both ups and downs. Imagine being lucky enough to have spotted and invested in Amazon back in 1997. You wouldn't want to have an itchy finger on the sell button after making tenfold your initial investment because you wouldn't want to miss out on the subsequent 100 fold return!

Cyclicals

Cyclicals are a class of stocks that are not suitable for all investors. These are companies that rise and fall with the economic cycle. Examples of cyclical companies/industries are in the Marriot Hotels, American Airlines, and General Motors. When a recession hits, cyclicals are the "canary in a coal mine", and are the first to suffer drops in revenue, earnings, and are more at risk of cutting their dividends. People are not going to buy a new car or take a vacation to Hawaii if they are concerned about losing their job. Cyclicals are also referred to as bell weather stocks because their earnings reports can be used as one of many economic indicators of where we are in an economic cycle. Many technology companies are also cyclical to some extent.

If you are unsure whether or not if a company is a cyclical, then take a look at its revenue and earnings history through the last recession, and see if it had a significant drop in revenue and earnings. Some companies such as those in the travel industry are obviously cyclical, but other companies such as industrials are not so obvious and it is only through digging into their earnings history through a recession that you can find out to what extent its business is cyclical (by seeing how much its earnings dropped on a % basis and the speed of its recovery through a recession). Investing in cyclicals can be profitable as long as you are aware of the risks involved, and time your purchase in them when they are in a downturn. If you don't have the stomach for volatile up and downswings, then you should stick with more conservative investments that may be more suitable for you such as blue chip stalwarts and dividend aristocrats.

Stalwarts

Stalwarts such as Wal-Mart and McDonald's are known as secular stocks because they are not necessarily tied or sensitive to the swings of the economic cycle. McDonald's can actually be regarded as an all-weather stock, because it can perform well in both times of economic expansion and contraction. Just look at how they performed during the Great Recession of '08-'09. McDonald's revenue and earnings grew during that time. Why? Because when times are tight, consumers will avoid spending a lot on high-end dining and be more in favor of low cost options such as McDonald's. The same can be said about Wal-Mart and movie theaters. In fact, during a recession, more families will shop at Wal-Mart as a low-cost provider of basic needs and rather than splurge luxury goods. A family may also opt to go with a far cheaper entertainment option of going to the movies rather than going on a tour of Europe.

Note that just because a company is not cyclical does not mean it is not without risk. All companies have inherent risk, otherwise the expected return of their price appreciation and dividends would not be higher than that of the risk-free Treasury bond rate. For example, even though McDonald's thrived through the Great Recession, it faced difficult challenges within its own industry in 2014-2015 from both a menu price and competitive offering standpoint. Consumers perceived the McDonald's brand to be staid and were flocking to new and hip fast food upstarts such as Shake Shack. But a global brand such as McDonald's with a strong balance sheet does not go the way of the dinosaur overnight and without a fight. They were quick to adapt to changing consumer tastes buy offering all-day breakfast and revamped its menu offerings that highlighted options for today's health conscious consumers. Sales were quickly re-invigorated and the stock bounced back.

They way that I like to think about it is that all companies, both big and small, are under siege to some extent and as an investor, you have to be comfortable with the idea of bearing risk for profit. What sets a good to great company from an average one is its financial muscle (solid balance sheet, with a BBB credit rating or higher), a solid brand which serves as a moat, and a strong management team with a track record of navigating rough seas.

Healthcare giant Johnson & Johnson is another example of a stalwart that is generally immune to recessions. On top of being in an industry that is recession-resistant, J&J also has a diversified line of products that touch nearly every consumer, from medical equipment used in hospitals, to pharmaceutical drugs that provide life-saving treatment, to over-the-counter household brand names such as Tylenol. And if that is not enough, J&J is just one of two companies to have an AAA credit rating from S&P, even higher than the credit rating of the U.S. Government. Having such an exemplary credit rating means that J&J has the balance sheet strength to weather severe economic hardships. I would liken an AAA credit rating to having a near 850 consumer credit score. Creditors view highly rated companies by S&P, Moody's, and Fitch as having low loan default risk, and are therefore willing to extend credit at the most attractive interest rates.

However, just because J&J is a high quality company does not mean it is investable at any price. At too high a valuation, an investment in J&J can be risky as a normalization in the share price from too high a valuation to a historically normal valuation (coming back down to earth) can result in significant losses. It may take years for the share price to eventually come back with normal growth rates in earnings. As everything comes with a risk versus rewards, even a high quality company can turn out to be a poor investment choice with little returns if purchased at significantly above fair value (see chapter on value investing).

While I do believe cyclical stocks can have a place in a portfolio if purchased at attractively low prices, I'm a much bigger fan of recession resistant stalwarts. To use a friend analogy, I would compare cyclical stocks to fair-weather friends. You can count on your fair-weather friends to come and join you for a beer and a good laugh when you're riding high, but they are never there for you when the times are tough. Don't get me wrong, there is nothing wrong with having a few fair-weather friends as long as you know what you are getting into and set the right expectations. For me personally, I'd rather have a strong group of all-weather friends that can be there for me even when times are tough.

Be Picky About What You Buy

Just like how you should be picky about who your closest friends are, you should also be picky about what stocks go into your portfolio. Here is a neat little trick when it comes to being picky. Before buying any stock, have the mindset that if you buy the stock, you will hold onto it forever and collect the dividends along the way. Something interesting happens when you have this mindset, because it sharpens your focus on not only what could go right with the stock, but more importantly, all that can go wrong with the stock. Questions that you may ask yourself would include: How would this company fare in a recession? How susceptible is this company to being disrupted by technology? Is this company over-leveraged? How strong of a competitive moat does this company have? What is the management track record for delivering shareholder value? Asking these tough questions helps you to filter out many stocks that are not suitable for long term investment.

I actually think that half of the stocks in the market are not suitable for the average retail investor. The reason is because many of the companies have too complex business models or are too risky for the retail investor to fully understand or diversify away the risk from. An example would be a small pharmaceutical company that is hinging its survival on the FDA approval of its drug. Unlike a large hedge fund or mutual fund, the retail investor does not have an army of analysts to do research on small and loosely followed companies. The lack of available research on these types of companies puts the retail investor at an inherent disadvantage compared to fund portfolio managers with greater resources for research.

Lastly, having the luxury to be picky comes only after you've evaluated a lot of stocks. The more stocks you evaluate and reject, the closer you get to honing in on your own investment methodology and finding the right ones that you would want for your portfolio. It is not uncommon for expert investors to evaluate 20 companies, and only pick one or two final candidates for investment based on their assessment of valuation, risk, and suitability.

CHAPTER 5: DIVIDENDS

Dividends are my favorite part of investing. Once a dividend is paid, it is yours to keep and unlike executive compensation, a dividend can never be clawed back by the company, its creditors, or the government. A dividend payment also prevents management from squandering that same money on potentially unwise pet projects or on lavish expenditures that destroy shareholder value. As John D. Rockefeller once famously put it: "The only thing that gives me pleasure is to see my dividend checks come in." While that is an exaggeration (I would hope more things can make you happy than dividends alone), it does stress the value that many investors place on receiving a regular dividend. For me, receiving a dividend represents the reciprocal relationship between myself as an investor and the business that is paying me for bearing the risk of ownership. The term, Dividend Growth Investors (DGI), represents are a class of investors that primarily buy companies that pay a safe and growing dividend.

A good way to find recession resistant stalwarts (or all-weather friends as I would call them) is to look for Dividend Aristocrats. This term is reserved for companies that have increased their dividend every year for at least the past 25 years. Making it to this exclusive club is no easy feat, as it demonstrates that the company has weathered multiple economic shocks (including the Great Recession) and interest rate cycles, all while rewarding their shareholders with increasing dividends each and every year.

Speaking of the Great Recession, I believe that proved to

be an excellent litmus test as some companies that were Dividend Aristocrats up to that point fell off the list because their business models came under too much stress during that difficult time, and they had to cut their dividends. If you want to be super selective, then you can look for Dividend Kings, which is a term reserved for companies that have increased their dividends every year for over 50 years! Lowe's and 3M are Dividend Kings and are household names because of the durability of their business models and strong management execution through many economic cycles.

If you can't find enough attractively low priced companies on the Dividend Aristocrats list, then you can build your own criteria based on the number of years that a company has increased its dividend. One of the first websites that I visit after finding an interesting stock is DividendChannel.com. There, you can enter the ticker symbol and find the dividend history for that company. One of the key focuses for me is how the dividend payments fared during the Great Recession. If they were frozen (remained flat) or mildly reduced, then I would not be too concerned if the stock is attractively priced and fits my other investment criteria (i.e. a low P/E ratio, good business prospects, solid balance sheet), but if they were suspended (reduced to 0) or drastically cut, then that is a major red flag for me. I would not consider investing in the latter unless if the underlying business model has fundamentally changed since then.

Just because a company has a good track record of paying dividends does not mean the dividend is safe. When evaluating companies for potential investment, I always ask myself "How vulnerable is the business model to disruption and can there be a reasonable expectation for the underlying business continue to grow for at least another 25 years?" If the answer is no to either question, then you should pass up that investment opportunity. Take Pitney Bowes, a former dividend aristocrat, for example. They make machines that take care of USPS Postage for you, and can be conveniently placed at your place of business so that you don't have to waste time going to the Post Office. The problem is that in the internet age, personal mail has become less and less relevant. I can't remember the last time I needed personal USPS service at the office since I pay all of my bills and correspond with my friends online. Pitney Bowe's business model has undoubtedly experienced weakness because of this sea change in consumer behavior and as a result, halved its quarterly dividend in 2013 from .375 per share to .188 per share, and cut again in 2019 to just .05 cents per share. Just like how one would do research on a car's reliability or "kicking its tires" before making a purchase, one should also question the durability of a company's business model and the safety and reliability of their dividends before making an investment in that company.

The Dividend Payout Ratio

The dividend payout ratio is a useful metric to measure the safety of the dividend. It is calculated by taking the latest annual dividend per share amount by the annual earnings per share. For example, if a company pays 50 cents per share each quarter, then the annualized dividend amount would be $2 per share. If the company's earnings for the year is $8, then the payout ratio is 25% (2 divided by 8), which is a very safe payout ratio. The remaining portion of earnings that the company does not pay out in dividends (i.e. $6 per share in this example) can be used by the company to build a cash cushion for difficult times, repurchase shares, repay debt, or pay for capital projects to maintain existing infrastructure or expand into new lines of businesses. Having a low payout ratio implies that the dividend safe and has a high margin of safety.

Companies that have a payout ratio of less than 60% are generally regarded as having a safe and well-covered dividend. Companies with payout ratios between 60% and 80% are considered to have a moderately safe dividend, and payout ratios above 80% are considered to be more at risk of a dividend cut if the business comes under pressure. Note that this is just a general rule of thumb rather than a one-size-fits-all approach. For example, net lease REITs such as Realty Income Corporation has a payout ratio above 80% that many consider to be safe, because it has a very high quality underlying revenue stream that comes from 10 year leases to mostly credit worth tenants under triple net arrangements (tenant is responsible for paying taxes, insurance, and maintenance). Note that for REITs, the payout ratio should be calculated based on dividends/Funds from Operations (FFO) rather than dividends/Earnings. Reason is because REITs are capital intensive (buildings) which incur high depreciation (a non-cash item) that greatly deflates earnings. FFO serves as a cash flow-centric metric that better represents the profitability of a REIT.

Debt Metrics

Other metrics that I like to use to measure dividend safety are the Debt to Ebitda and the Interest Coverage ratio. The first one, Debt to Ebitda, is calculated by taking a company's debt minus its assets, divided by its annual earnings before interest, taxes, depreciation, and amortization (Ebitda). The resulting ratio provides a measure of how leveraged a company is from a cash flow standpoint. One can think of it as a theoretical way of measuring how many years it would take a company to pay off all of its net debt if it devoted all of its cash flows to that effort. Note that I said theoretical, because it is unrealistic for a company to not pay any interest and taxes. But nonetheless, it is a good metric to use as it serves as a normalized debt metric for comparison across companies and industries.

I prefer using the Debt to Ebitda ratio compared to other debt metrics such as Debt to Assets and Debt to Equity. Reason is because Assets and Equity are impacted by non-cash items such as depreciation and goodwill, which can easily distort these metrics and may make a company appear to be in better or worse financial shape that it actually is compared to its peers. The debt to cash flow (ebitda) nature of this metric is especially helpful to assessing how safe a company's dividend is. Generally, I would regard a Debt to Ebitda of less than 2.5 as being safe, between 2.5 and 3.5 as being moderate, and above 3.5 as being higher risk. However, as with all metrics, this is just a general rule that can vary across industries.

For example, the utility companies are notoriously capital intensive, requiring them to continuously spend on upgrading and maintaining their infrastructure. Utilities therefore will have higher Debt to Ebitda ratios than other industries, but their cash flows are very safe compared to that of other industries. Utilities are considered a non-discretionary basic good, and is an expense that households will prioritize over other discretionary goods. It is therefore acceptable for Utilities to have a higher Debt to Ebitda due to the durability of their cash flows, as long as you are mindful of how any one utility's Debt to Ebitda compares to other utilities and the industry norm. Credit ratings agencies such as Moody's will do much of the upfront analysis heavy lifting for you, so it's important to check out the company's assigned credit rating as a starting point. My recommendation is an assigned rating of BBB or higher.

The Interest Coverage ratio is a measure of how much buffer a company has in servicing its interest payments. It is calculated by taking the company's annual free cash flow (FCF), which is readily obtained from the cash flow statement, and dividing it by the annual interest expense, also readily obtained on the cash flow statement. For example, an interest coverage ratio of 8x implies that a company generates 8 times the amount of cash required to service its debt (interest payments). Creditors generally have debt covenants that require a company to maintain a certain amount of buffer in its ability to service its debt. If a debt covenant is breached, then the creditor has the right to call back all of its debt immediately, which could trigger a liquidity crisis for the company as it needs to raise cash to pay back the debt. That could include among other things, a dividend cut and/or dilutive equity issuances (i.e. sell more shares to the public, thereby decreasing the value of existing shares). Having a high Interest Coverage Ratio compared to peers is a good sign that the company is on solid financial footing and is prepared to weather an economic downturn.

A company's ability to maintain moderate to low levels of debt is essential to ensuring the safety of its dividend and its business model. Having low amounts of debt relative to industry peers is what enables certain companies to weather and survive industry headwinds and recessions whereas others cannot. Companies with low debt also have the advantage of being able to take advantage of adverse economic conditions by acquiring competitors with weaker balance sheets at an attractively low price. Take for example Simon Property Group (SPG), a best in class operator of Class A Malls. SPG had a strong balance sheet heading into the Great Recession, and was able to take advantage of the opportunity to buy high quality competitors with weak balance sheets at bargain prices. SPG emerged from the Great Recession with an even stronger portfolio of assets, thanks to its conservative capital structure and opportunistic use of funds during the recession.

Non-Dividend Paying Companies

Companies that do not pay dividends tend to be ones that are in growth phase and need to reserve funds for future expansion. It is not uncommon for technology companies to go 20+ years until their businesses have fully matured before paying a dividend. Cisco Systems, for example, did not start paying a dividend until 26 years after it was founded. Amazon and Google have the cash flow to pay a dividend but reserves that cash for continued expansion and reinvestment into their existing lines of business. Berkshire Hathaway famously does not pay a dividend because Warren Buffett feels that he can continue to generate a high ROI for shareholders by reinvesting into the company and feels that this method is more tax efficient for shareholders since profits cannot be taxed twice at the corporate level. A dividend is essentially taxed twice – once as profits at the corporate level, and again after the dividend is received by the shareholder at the personal tax level.

Personally, I prefer to invest in companies that pay dividends because I like the idea having an extra recurring stream of income, and being able to pay my bills with that income. Imagine if my portfolio only contained non-dividend paying stocks. I would then have to count on just the capital gains in the share price, which is subject to wild swings based on whims of the market. I would have to sell some shares if I needed to raise extra cash, and selling those shares could come at a great opportunity cost of missing out on future gains in those shares. Also, even great companies can be undervalued for an extended period of time during an economic downturn, a time you need extra income the most. Dividend income helps you weather the tough times and mitigates the need for you to raise additional cash through selling undervalued holdings. To put it simply, you are getting paid in both good and bad times.

Start Small, Grow Big

It may seem daunting at first to think of being able to cover living expenses such as a mortgage/rent, utilities, insurance, etc... with dividend income and to that, I would say start small. Rome was not built in a day, and neither should your portfolio. Recall the story of Grace Groner, who started with just 3 shares of Abbott Labs, and ended with a portfolio worth $7 Million, all through the power of compounding. Think of it this way

– you've decided to allocate $500 for investment per month, and find an attractively priced company that is paying a 4% annual dividend yield. That investment will yield you $240 annually (500 x .04 x 12 months) and you've just covered the cost of gas for 60 roundtrip commutes to work (assuming $4 per roundtrip). Or better yet, if you drive an electric vehicle and get free-charging at your company, then you've just covered 32 discounted lunches at your company café (assuming $7.50 per meal). Plus, if you re-invest your dividends and get a dividend increase next year, your income stream will grow exponentially. My point is that with time and the power of compounding on your side, you can readily grow a small and modest portfolio income stream into one that adds a great amount of financial security for you and your family.

Many companies and brokerages offer DRIP plans, which stands for Dividend Reinvestment Plan. Under these plans, dividends paid by a company are automatically reinvested into buying additional shares of that company. This automatic reinvestment of dividends eliminates the need to pay brokerage commissions. Do note however, that in a taxable (non-retirement) account, you are responsible for coming up with the 15% dividend tax when taxes are due (20% tax for high income households). When you take the dividend payment in cash instead of automatic reinvestment, you have the flexibility to set aside the taxed portion of the dividend for the IRS come tax time. You also the flexibility keep the cash and wait for opportune times to invest in either the same company or other companies when they are attractively mispriced.

Speaking of dividend reinvestment, there is a useful website: dividendchannel.com/drip-returns-calculator where you can plug a stock ticker symbol and see what the total return would be with and without dividend reinvestment. Additionally, you can compare different stocks against one another on this website.

In closing, dividends are a great way to provide an alternate reliable source of income for you. When choosing dividend

paying companies, be mindful of the following:
1.) Underlying business model (i.e. is it vulnerable to a recession, and is it vulnerable to technological disruption over the next 25 years)
2.) The payout ratio
3.) Credit metrics (i.e. have a minimum of a BBB credit rating)
4.) The dividend track record (did it weather a recession)
5.) Valuation: P/E Ratio (P/FFO for REITs)
6.) Debt Metrics (Debt to Ebitda and Interest Coverage ratios)

CHAPTER 6: MOATS MATTER

The concept of an economic moat refers to company's ability to withstand adversity. Just like how a castle is backed by a strong army behind its fortified walls and a water moat filled with alligators, a company's moat serves as a deterrent to competitors seeking to chip away at its profit margin. Say you've discovered an appealing fruit from France that really catches on in America, and you're the first one to grow it, enabling you to charge a high price for it, and thereby earn a high profit margin. Inevitably, a competitor will utter the phrase: "your margin is my opportunity", and will not only grow the same fruit, but also heavily invest in resources that will make growing, harvesting, and transporting the fruit more efficient. He will also charge a slightly lower price to capture market share away from you.

Soon, more competitors will join in on the fray, and what was once a profitable business quickly becomes a price war in a race to the bottom. The reason for why this happened is because the initial business had no moat due to the commoditized nature of the underlying product. Unless if you have patent protection for growing this fruit, there is nothing to prevent competitors from entering and taking profit share away from you.

An example of a company that does have a moat is General Mills. Imagine if you had the resources to acquire General Mills. Do you think the owners would be willing to part ways with their ownership if you simply offered to buy all of the physical assets of the company? The answer is no because they would charge you a hefty premium. That premium would be for the intangibles for the company otherwise known as goodwill. Among the intangibles include the branding such as that of their top cereal brand: Cheerios. Even if a new upstart competitor made an identical breakfast cereal to Cheerios, they would not be able to charge the same price for it because consumers will generally go for a trusted brand that they are familiar and comfortable with. Having trusted and reputable brands is something that General Mills has built upon over decades through heavy investments in advertising and strategic product placement in grocery stores. There is a reason for why many brands are household names, and that is not something that can be taken down overnight. Another moat is the costly infrastructure, distribution network, and trusted relationships with grocers that General Mills has built up over many years. All of these factors form a moat that make it very difficult for a new entrant to overcome.

CHAPTER 7: VALUE INVESTING

Taking a value-minded approach towards investing and combining that with a long-term buy-and-hold mindset is what I believe to be a winning strategy. There are many individual retail investors who trade in and out of stocks with the goal of beating the market. That is a common attitude that many people have towards the stock market and you probably have a friend, neighbor, or relative who have that approach to the market. I would say that while beating the market is definitely a good thing, it should not be the overriding focus for most investors. Reason is because when you are focused only on beating the market, your mind will inherently shift to engage in riskier behavior, such as chasing momentum stocks, or the next hot IPO that everyone is talking about. In addition, you would also be less inclined to hold onto your stocks and more inclined to sell them at the first sign of weakness.

Let's say you are a star trader who racks up a lot of profitable trades, and those trades look great on your brokerage statement showing that you have beaten the market index. However, come tax time, you may find that those gains aren't so great after taking out the capital gains taxes that you will need to pay. Short term capital gains (on stocks held for less than a year) are taxed at your ordinary income rate, and long term capital gains are taxed at 20%, 15%, or 0% based on your income bracket. Don't underestimate the ability for capital gains taxes to eat into your gains.

Rather than aiming to beat the market, I recommend

aiming to minimize your risk by taking a value-minded investing approach. This means buying companies whenever they are attractively low priced, so long as they fit the qualities mentioned in other chapters of this book, namely: companies with strong moats, an investment credit rating (BBB or higher), and a solid track record of rewarding shareholders with increasing dividends. Taking a value-minded approach towards investing has been a ticket to long term wealth for many people, and that means one must approach the market with the right expectation of not trying to become rich overnight.

There is a company behind every ticker symbol with 4 key groups: shareholders, creditors, employees, and customers. Within each company is a delicate interplay between these four groups with the goal of serving a need (employees and customers) and earning a profit for the stakeholders (shareholders and creditors). The stock price at which a company is trading at is *a value* that the market is assigning at any given time based on its assessment of perceived risks, sustainability, and growth of a company's business model (i.e. the interplay between the four groups).

Note that I use chose my words above carefully by saying "a value" rather than "the value". That's because a company's stock price is only the representation of the last trade that took place between a buy and seller in the market. That price is not necessarily a reflection of the true intrinsic value of the company because many buyers and sellers could just be sitting on the sidelines, waiting for a better price at which to buy or sell. This disconnect results in many companies being either overvalued or undervalued and this mispricing can last for an extended period of time. Often times, and comically, the only time when some stocks are fairly valued are when they are on their way from an undervaluation to an overvaluation, and vice versa.

It is also not uncommon for stocks to have wild swings in its share price within a single trading day. If a stock ends up trading at the same market close price as it did at the market open, one may come to the wrong conclusion that nothing really happened to the stock in the trading day, when in reality the opposite was true and the stock could have had a wild plus and minus 2% differential equaling a total 4% swing. Imagine that you owned a farm, the market is giving you a constant stream of quotes with this month's quoted price being 10% lower than last month's quote. You as the owner know the intrinsic value of your farm and would probably think the market quotes are just plain silly half the time as being too high or too low.

The inherent advantage that you have as a long term investor over the short term investors and traders is that you can choose to ignore the market when the price does not work to your advantage, and to take advantage when a stock is grossly mispriced. As a buy and hold type investor, I like to buy in small lots when I perceive a stock to be mispriced. Why small lots? Because with small lots, I have the flexibility to buy more and average down my cost on shares if the shares become even cheaper. When a stock experiences weakness in price, rarely will you catch an absolute bottom just on a single purchase, so I'm prepared to make multiple smaller purchases as an alternative to trying to catch an absolute bottom in one fell swoop. In other words, just because a stock is cheap does not mean it can't get cheaper.

Valuation Metrics

The investment standard for valuing a company is the P/E ratio (or P/FFO for REITs). The 'P' stands for the price per share and the 'E' stands for earnings per shares. Earnings represents the cash flow from operations that a company generates from its businesses, less non-cash charges such as depreciation on its capital assets. So for example, if a company's stock price is $24 per share, and the annual earnings is $2, then the P/E ratio is equal to 12 (24/2 = 12).

Note that for REITs, P/FFO should be used and the reason is because REITs are a capital intensive business (physical buildings) and take large depreciation charges (a non-cash item) that greatly reduce earnings. FFO (Funds from Operations) is a better measure of "earnings" for REITS because it adds back the non-cash charges such as depreciation. Therefore P/FFO is a better measure of the profitability of a REIT versus P/E.

I typically think of companies that have a P/E ratio below 12.5 as being undervalued, between 12.5 and 17.5 as fairly valued, and above 17.5 as overvalued. The typical standard for fair value is a P/E ratio of 15. Note that this is just a general rule of thumb and does not necessarily apply to all situations. For example, for a company in a growth industry that is increasing its earnings by 15% YoY, then a P/E ratio of 18 could be an undervaluation because after a few years of 20% growth would mean that today's price at 18 times earnings would have a P/E of just 10 after a few years when the earnings denominator grows bigger. Likewise, a company with a P/E ratio of 12 but is suffering -10% YoY earnings declines is not so cheap, because today's price of 12 times earnings could mean a P/E ratio of 18 in a few years as the earnings denominator contracts.

Another metric that can be used as a complement to P/E ratio (for non-REITs) is Price to Free Cash Flow (P/FCF). Reason is because sometimes a company may need to take a one-time goodwill impairment charge that significantly and negatively impacts earnings, but is not considered to be recurring in the nature of its business. Goodwill represents the amount of money that is used to pay to acquire another company that is in excess of the fair value of the acquired company's assets. Goodwill therefore represents intangibles such as the acquired company's brand value and cost efficiencies (or synergies) that can be gained from the acquisition.

PEG Ratio

A good complement to the P/E ratio is the PEG ratio, which stands for Price to Earnings Growth. Similar to the P/E ratio, the PEG ratio is a measure of Price to Earnings, but also includes an Earnings Growth component as well. The PEG formula is calculated as follows: (P/E) / Earnings Growth. For example if a company is trading at $20 per share, and its annual earnings is $1.25 per share, then its P/E Ratio is 16 (20/1.25 = 16). If its expected earnings growth rate is 15%, then its PEG ratio is 1.07 (16/15 = 1.07).

Generally, I would recommend stocks that have a PEG ratio under 2, giving consideration to other qualities and financial metrics as well. Do note that quality of the PEG ratio is only as good as the inputs used. While Price and Earnings per share are straightforward and accurate to the best of everyone's knowledge, Earnings Growth is more arbitrary and tied to analyst expectations. Generally speaking, a widely followed stock with many analysts following it will have a more accurate Earnings Growth estimate (think wisdom of the crowd) compared to a loosely followed stock with only one or two analyst estimates.

Goodwill

Goodwill is reviewed by the corporate accounting department and its auditors every year for impairment, and sometimes, they find that the acquired brand value and cost synergies may not be as much as originally paid for at time of acquisition. This would result in the company taking a goodwill impairment charge. Companies that take a goodwill impairment will see its earnings take a significant hit, which thereby heavily skews the P/E ratio upward (lower earnings results in a higher P/E multiple), thereby making the company look rather expensive at its current share price. The P/FCF ratio takes out the non-cash charges like goodwill impairment and can be used as a complement to the P/E ratio in assessing the run-rate profitability of a business from a cash flow perspective. Note that if a company is consistently taking goodwill impairment charges, then that could be indicatively of a greater fundamental problem at the company in which it is constantly overpaying to acquire target companies and thereby wasting precious shareholder resources.

Questioning the Market Price

The job of a value investor is to be skeptical of market prices and to take a conservative approach in determining whether if a company's stock price truly deserves a high valuation by asking the questions – Is the growth likely to continue or is the market being irrationally exuberant about the company's prospects? How big a moat does this company have and how vulnerable is it to hungry competitors who also want a piece of the action? Likely for companies with a low valuation, the value investor should be skeptical and ask – Is this company truly suffering a permanent impairment to its business or is the market being overly pessimistic over its prospects for correcting the issues for a turnaround?

The point is that the P/E ratio should be the start of the analysis rather than the end. It should warrant further research and digging by you as a value investor rather than being the sole deciding factor in whether or not you choose to invest. Investing is more an art than a science. There is no such thing as a magic formula financial ratio that holds to key to riches. If that were the case, then the smartest mathematicians in the world would also be all the richest people, which is not the case. Likewise, there is never a 100% guarantee that an investment will work out because investors are human, and the companies are run by humans who are not infallible.

Margin of Safety

The concept of a margin of safety applies to the physical world in the same way that it does to investing in stocks. If you are driving a truck weighing 10,000 pounds, you wouldn't feel comfortable with driving across a bridge that was designed to just withstand 10,000 pounds. You would want the bridge to be able to withstand 25,000 pounds. That extra 15,000 pounds is your margin of safety. The same idea applies to value investing. All else being equal, investing in a stock with a high P/E ratio is generally riskier than a stock with a low P/E ratio. That's because a stock with a high P/E ratio is termed what is called "priced for perfection", meaning that the market has priced the stock as if it can do no wrong and continue its impressive growth trajectory into the foreseeable future without any issues. There is no margin of safety with investing in a stock that is "priced for perfection" because any number of factors can cause the thesis to break, and when that happens the share price will be overly punished due to a drastic change in the investor sentiment on the company stock. It is often these times that create the best buying opportunities, as it enables value investors to come in and buy otherwise good companies at bargain basement prices, as long as they believe the management can work through the issues that are currently affecting the company.

Often times, I would hear people talk about how risky it is to invest in a certain stock that had fallen to a P/E ratio of 10. To that, I would say it was risky to invest in the company when it was trading at a much higher P/E ratio, when it was priced for perfection. At least now, with a P/E of 10, the stock price has come back down to earth and possibly overly-punished, leaving a margin of safety for value minded investors. Of course, this is just an illustrative example and as mentioned earlier in this chapter, I'm not recommending anyone to invest in a stock on basis of a low P/E ratio alone. Due diligence and judgment is warranted to determine whether if the headwinds are short-term or permanent in nature.

With so many on Wall Street focused on the short-term results rather than the long term, I believe that retail investors have an inherent advantage in the form of a time arbitrage. Wall Street hedge funds and mutual funds are bound to reporting periodic results (often quarterly) to their investors, and so many of them are focused on the short term. If a stock is overly punished due to one quarter's earnings miss, that gives retail investors with a longer time horizon a chance to come in and buy up shares on the cheap.

Insider Purchases

Insider purchases are another gauge that can be used to identify value opportunities. Insider purchases refer to open market stock purchases made by corporate officers and directors. As the saying goes: "There are a number of reasons for why someone would sell stock, but only one reason for someone to buy stock, and that is to make money". Insider purchases are generally a good sign that the officer or director making the purchase feels that the company shares are undervalued and is willing to risk their own money to buy shares. This is especially positive considering that most corporate officers and directors already receive annual stock grants as part of their compensation packages. Therefore, to see them purchase shares with their own money in addition to the shares they already receive as part of their compensation package is a good sign.

It also feels good when you buy stock in a company that you like at a price lower than what insiders had recently paid. This means that you got a bargain price below the price at which the insider thought was already a bargain. Just be aware that an insider purchase should not be taken as a standalone reason for you to also buy stock. In rare cases, insiders will make token open market stock purchases only to give the appearance of an alignment of interest. Insiders are also not infallible, and could be overly enthusiastic about their company's business prospects. As with all other principles discussed in this book, this combined with other considerations should help you make an informed decision on whether or not to invest in a particular stock.

Share Buybacks

Publicly traded companies have many levers to boost profitability, whether it be from expanding market share, driving cost efficiencies, or raising prices. These are common methods that all companies, both public and private have as their options. However, one inherent advantage that public companies have over private ones is their ability to buy back shares at the prevailing market price. This is something that private companies cannot easily replicate. If a private company is owned by multiple parties, it can be an arduous process to "buyout" one of the parties, requiring the consensus of all owners of the company. For a public company, "buying out" shareholders by buying back shares that shareholders are willingly selling on the open market is relatively easier, as all that is required is a share buyback authorization by the Board of Directors.

Buying back shares can be accretive to shareholders if done at an attractive value (low P/E). For example, if a stock is unfairly punished by an overly pessimistic to a low P/E ratio of just 10, then every dollar that the company buys back generates a permanent 10 cent (or 10%) Return on Investment for the remaining shareholders (1/10 = 10%). That means that if a company is not able to generate a 10% ROI (in this case) from putting the cash to use on its business operations, then buying back shares is a simple and guaranteed way of generating a 10% ROI for shareholders.

Recall that P/E is price-per-share divided by earnings-per-share. When shares are bought back by the company, earnings-per-share gets a boost because the number of shares outstanding (also known as the float) is reduced. Since earnings-per-share has increased due to the aforementioned reduction in share count, the price-per-share would then need to increase to get to the same P/E ratio as before. So basically and with all else equal, the remaining shareholders' shares are more valuable (higher share price) because the number of shares outstanding (the float) has been reduced. This can be especially rewarding to dividend growth investors because after a buyback, the company has fewer shares on which it needs to pay dividends, therefore giving the company the financial flexibility to increase the dividends to the remaining shareholders.

A Market for Stocks Rather than the Stock Market

Many people will think that all stocks are overpriced when the S&P 500 index is at or near an all-time high. While the stock market as a whole can be expensive, the same is not true for all stocks. The reason is because the S&P 500 index is a weighted measure based on the market cap of its component companies. That means outperformance by leading companies on the index such as Amazon, Apple, and Alphabet carries an outsized influence over the performance of the entire index and can mask flat or underperformance in the share prices of relatively smaller companies. Rather than thinking of it as a stock market, think of it as a market of stocks. If you follow enough stocks and expose yourself to well-thought out research (see chapter on paying for investment advice), you will find that there are always bargains to be had in the market, whether if we are in a bull market or bear market.

I will close this chapter with this saying, which I believe represents the heart of value investing: "the stock market is designed to transfer wealth from the active to the patient". What this means is to exercise patience with your holdings. As long as the initial thesis for your purchase has not changed and you don't need the money for other uses, then don't get the itch to sell. If you sell, then in the best case, you will have to pay taxes on your capital gains, and in the worst case, you will sell it for a loss. Secondly, the aforementioned saying also applies to exercising patience when it comes to waiting for an attractive entry point to buy stocks when they are grossly mispriced. Adopting this mindset along with fundamental analysis of the business can help you minimize your losses while maximizing your opportunities for success. Even if you end up with losers in your portfolio, with time and patience the winners will more than make up for them many times over.

CHAPTER 8: DIVERSIFICATION

Same as how strong companies have an economic moat protecting them, an investment portfolio should also have a moat protecting itself in the form of diversification. All companies are under siege in one form or another. While you should invest in companies with strong moats, there are no guarantees that any one company, no matter how strong, will not succumb to competitive, economic, or industry pressures at least in the short to medium time frame. A well-diversified portfolio with 20 to 40 companies can help you mitigate a lot of risks. For example, let's say you own a stalwart in the fast food industry but suddenly the company falls victim to a black swan event such as mass beef recall that would take it 6 months to a year to manage through. Having another company in an unrelated sector such as 3M can greatly help contain losses and disruption to your portfolio.

Diversification should be a byproduct of expanding your horizons in looking for attractively priced companies across different industries. In other words, you should not diversify just for the sake of diversifying. This means that a portfolio in its early stages may be concentrated in just a few well-researched holdings and it may take years before additional companies can be purchased at attractive enough prices to warrant adding to the portfolio. Patience is key. When you diversify just for diversification's sake, then you may actually be "di-worsifying" your portfolio by adding positions that are overpriced and/or riskier and this can actually be a drag on your portfolio's performance.

Grow Wealthy With Stocks

Also, not all holdings have to have the same percentage weighting in your portfolio. Some of your largest holdings could be your favorite ones that you closely follow and understand very well. You may also find that some of the biggest holdings in your portfolio are the ones you bought early on, and had grown over the years through price appreciation. I've heard all too often from people who trimmed large positions in their portfolio simply because they have grown too big through price appreciation. I don't recommend trimming positions for that reason, because as long as the underlying fundamentals of the business is not broken, you should just hold onto the position and let the appreciation and dividends ride. Besides, seeing an uninterrupted growing position also serves as a fun measure of your stock picking successes and a reminder of how to identify successful future opportunities elsewhere. On top of all this, you don't need to pay taxes on any unrealized gains by simply holding onto your position.

Small positions are a good way to be engaged in a company without committing fully committing (and risking) a lot of capital. Sometimes you may be short on investable capital, but have found a company worthy of your investment and decide to open up a starter position. Either way, having a position in a company, no matter how small, sets up your mind as having a vested interest in a company and keeps you engaged in news and earnings about the company such that you may eventually want to commit more investment capital to it when the time is right. Sure, you can follow a company even if you're not invested in it and I do that all the time, but you will never be truly care about that company unless if you have some skin in the game by committing capital to it, no matter how small.

In addition, starting small gives you the advantage of picking up shares at opportune times. It is rare, when you find an attractively priced stock that it won't drop further. In many cases, it will fluctuate, drop, fluctuate, and perhaps drop some more. Many of my holdings started out small and ended up growing big through my interest in the company, and steady accumulation of shares whenever it is attractively priced.

How Many Stocks Should I Hold?

What is the optimal number of stocks to hold in a diversified portfolio? That question is often asked in investment circles. Some would say that 5 stocks is enough whereas others would say 50. I would say a minimum of 10 stocks should be held in a diversified portfolio, but I wouldn't set any hard cap on the maximum number of stocks in a portfolio. The reason is because diversification does not necessarily have to be just across industries, but also across companies within an industry. While more than one company in the same industry may not reduce industry-specific risks, it does reduce company-specific risks.

Say for example, you are able to acquire shares in Pfizer at a value price. Should Pfizer then represent the entire pharmaceutical sector of your portfolio? The answer is that it does not have to. While Pfizer is indeed a blue-chip company and a good representative of the pharma industry, it could have a very different growth, risk, and valuation profile than another pharmaceutical company. What if Pfizer hits a rough patch in drug development or from a failed acquisition? If you are able to buy another blue-chip pharma company such as AmGen at an attractive price (perhaps at a different point in time), then you will have greatly reduced any company-specific risk in Pfizer.

Also, what if Pfizer and your other portfolio holdings are not trading at a price with a sufficient margin of safety? (see chapter on valuation) You should be willing to add another company to your portfolio so long as it fits your investment criteria and has a margin of safety. If the new addition is purchased at an attractively low price, then you would effectively be incubating this holding for long term gains, while getting paid a dividend along the way. As this process repeats itself, and if you hold onto your stocks as long as your initial investment thesis for buying the company is not broken, then you could find yourself with a very diversified portfolio of stocks. Diversification is not just about mitigating risks, it is also a natural byproduct of continuously hunting for high quality companies that can be purchased at value prices.

Invest Conservatively, but Think Like a Venture Capitalist

You've probably heard the following refrain from the Venture Capital world about how if you invest in 10 startups, 5 of them will fail, 2-4 of them will produce low to average returns, and 1 will be successful enough to pay for all of them. I'm not a fan of investing in startups because I don't like the idea of losing my money on any investment, but I do think individual investors can apply the VC mindset by spreading risk across conservatively managed blue-chip companies when purchased at value prices. Most expert investors will go in on an investment if after their assessment on the business and price/value, they feel that they have a *reasonably good* chance of success, and when they diversify, they spread out their risk of loss, and increase their chances for a *good overall outcome*. If you make enough investments, then inevitably you will run into one that does not work out, but keep in mind that the most that you can lose in an investment is 100% of your invested capital, whereas there is no ceiling on how much you can earn from a profitable investment as the sky is the limit.

For many buy and hold value investors, the winners will more than pay for the losers. For example, imagine if many years ago you had invested an equal amount in just two companies. One of the companies turned out to be a dud and you lost 100% of your principal, but the other company was Microsoft. The initial optics of having only a 50% win rate may seem bad, but the huge gains you earn from Microsoft more than made up for your losses. I hope you understand that this was a rather extreme example of investing in 2 companies at the opposite ends of the reward spectrum. The point that I am making is that when you invest for value in a diversified basket of stocks, you maximize your chances for a good to great overall outcome.

CHAPTER 9: RISK VS REWARD

On the risk vs reward spectrum, the low risk assets such as Bonds will give the lowest reward (low yield) compared to preferred and common stock, which are supposed to yield higher returns (or else why would an investor be willing to bear the additional risk of being lower on the capital stack). Do note, however, that this is just general rule of thumb. For example, an investment in a junk bond (high risk of default) would probably net the investor a high yield of return in exchange for the high risk whereas an investment in the common stock in an AAA-rated rated company can net a lower rate of return in exchange for the low risk.

Alpha

An investment term that often gets mentioned in the financial press is 'alpha', and that is worth mentioning here. Alpha lies at the heart of the concept of risk versus reward. Before understanding what alpha is, we must first understand the 'risk free rate'. The 'risk free rate' is generally regarded as whatever % yield that U.S. Treasury Bonds are offering. In this case, we'll use the 10 year Treasury rate. Because the U.S. Government is generally regarded as never going to default on its debt obligations, the % yield on the 10 year Treasury is regarded as the 'risk free rate'. Alpha refers to the % return on investment that exceeds the risk free rate, hence the concept of investors bearing risk for profit. If for example, an investor purchased a corporate bond paying 5% interest, and the 10 year Treasury yield is 3%, then that investor will have generated 2% in alpha. Hence the next time you hear of someone saying "generating alpha", you'll know that they are referring to earning a % return on investment greater than the risk free Treasury rate. Generally speaking, the higher the risk that an investor assumes (i.e. investing in stock), the higher the alpha and expected return, and the lower the risk (i.e. bonds) the lower the alpha and expected return.

Bonds

The stakeholders of a company can be broken into two groups: shareholders and bondholders. This structure is what is also referred to as the capital stack, because there is a hierarchy in the order of payment in the event the company files for a bankruptcy. Bonds are senior to equity in the capital stack, meaning that in a bankruptcy, bondholders get to claim the assets of the company first, and shareholders get only the remainder. In the case of an overleveraged company, shareholders may be left with nothing. There is a hierarchy even within the bond structure in the form of senior secured (bonds secured by real assets) versus unsecured creditors. Unsecured creditors are senior to shareholders but junior to senior secured creditors. I would compare unsecured creditors to your credit card company, which has no direct claim over your assets and senior secured creditors to the first lien mortgage company which has a claim to your house, a hard asset.

One class of bonds that are helpful from a tax perspective are municipal bonds or "munis". Munis refer to bonds issued by state and local government agencies to fund public works projects. The benefit to owning munis is that the interest income generated from them are exempt from federal taxes. If you buy munis issued by your own state, then that income is exempt from both federal and state taxes. Do keep in mind that while the interest portion is not subject to federal and/or state income taxes, the capital gains portion is subject to taxes. The higher the tax income bracket you belong to, the more tax advantaged benefit you can get from the interest portion of a muni.

Preferred Stock

Likewise on the equity side, there can also be a hierarchy in the form of preferred and common stock. Preferred stock are a hybrid between a bond and a stock in the sense that it pays a fixed % dividend like a bond but is traded on the stock exchange like a stock. Preferred shares are senior to common shares but are junior to bonds in the event of a bankruptcy. Also preferred share dividends are safer than common share dividends as a company is required to suspend the common dividend before preferred share dividends can be eliminated. Cumulative preferred shares have added protection in that in the event preferred share dividends are suspended due to financial difficulty, the company must eventually pay back all of its missed preferred share dividends unless if the company goes bankrupt.

So what are the drawbacks of owning preferred shares? As mentioned earlier, preferred shares give fixed payments like bonds, so there are no dividend increases on preferred shares like there are on common shares. Also, preferred shares are callable by the company on a certain date, meaning that those preferred dividends will not necessarily continue into perpetuity. Lastly, preferred shares are more susceptible to interest rate risk because of its fixed payment bond-like quality. If interest rates rise, the "alpha" (the % above the risk free rate) generated on preferred shares will diminish and the price of preferred shares will fall. In an inflationary environment, the company may choose to not redeem its preferred shares on the callable date. A 6% yield on a preferred share may have been appealing when the 10 year treasury rate is at 2% (4% Alpha: 6% - 2%), but not very appealing if investors can get a much safer risk-free treasury rate at 5% (1% Alpha: 6% - 5%).

So when is a good time to buy preferred shares? In a rising interest rate environment, you will most likely see the prices of preferred shares drop below their par value (usually $25). The par value is the amount that the issuing company needs to pay you if it wants to redeem the preferred share. So if a the price of preferred shares drop to $20 in a rising rate environment, then purchasing those shares will give you a $5 upside if and when the company redeems the preferred shares. In addition, you are getting a higher preferred dividend yield buy purchasing the shares at $20 than $25. This is a solid opportunity for investors who want stable income with no dividend increase upside, but also limited dividend downside risk compared to the same company's common stock. If for example you just want to ensure that you have a steady stream of cash to fund your fixed monthly mortgage payment, then preferred stock dividends could be a solid choice to fulfill that need.

Why Invest in Common Stock?

So why would anyone want to buy common stock given the safer alternatives mentioned above? The answer is simple: there is opportunity for unlimited upside with common stock. The return on investment for bonds and preferred stock are capped, whereas the sky is the limit for equity both in capital appreciation and dividend increases. Common shareholders are the most important constituency for any public corporation, because only shareholders have voting power whereas bondholders do not. Most public corporations have investor relations dedicated to answering questions from shareholders and the quarterly and annual earnings reports are all geared towards shareholders.

Bonds, when used prudently and effectively, are an efficient source of capital for companies to use to invest into the business for the benefit of shareholders. While I do believe that short – medium term bonds have a place in any portfolio for stability (long term bonds are more subject to interest rate risk), the equity portion of the portfolio is what enables long-term wealth to be achieved.

CHAPTER 10: MUTUAL FUNDS

For many people, their only stock market investment is in mutual funds in their company sponsored 401(k) retirement plans. While mutual funds can be a good passive way to invest in the market, it is not what I am referring to when I talk about engaged investing as I mentioned earlier in this book. Reason is because mutual funds contain hundreds if not thousands of companies, and when you invest in a fund, you are not really engaged in the events surrounding the company. For example, if you buy an S&P 500 index fund, would you be able to name the #89th company and what their latest earnings were? Also, nobody is going to tell their friends and family about how excited they are about Coca-Cola's newest health drink when they are invested in it through a mutual fund.

Don't get me wrong, investing in mutual funds, namely low-cost index funds are a good way to build long-term wealth, and even Warren Buffett wants his heirs to put their inheritance in a low-cost S&P 500 index fund. But there is a reason an investor such as Buffett does not invest mutual funds himself, and that is because he wants to be engaged in knowing the goods and services that each of his individual investments provide and to be able to pick up investments at attractively low prices. When buying a mutual fund, you are buying a basket of stocks, some of which are undervalued, and others that are overvalued. For this reason, it is nearly impossible to take a value-minded approach to investing in mutual funds.

A drawback of mutual funds, namely the actively managed funds, is that when there is a big market sell-off, the fund manager may be forced to liquidate the portfolio's stock holdings at rock bottom prices if there are not enough cash reserves to meet the flood of client redemptions. This puts the fund's long term performance at a disadvantage because it handicaps the fund manager's ability to buy stocks at cheap valuations. While there are some talented fund managers out there that do very well for their clients, the inherent fee structure coupled with reasons such as the one stated above make it difficult for most funds to beat the average market index.

Today, there are hundreds of mutual funds to choose from, in nearly every imaginable category: small cap, mid cap, large cap, consumer staples, energy, technology, utilities, and industrials, to name a few. If you do find yourself having to invest mutual funds, as in the case of most company sponsored 401(k) plans, then I would recommend that you take full advantage of the company match and pick low-fee index funds.

CHAPTER 11: SEEKING AND PAYING FOR INVESTMENT ADVICE

One of the greatest investment lessons that I have learned over time is to be willing to seek out and advice, and pay for it if deemed from a worthy and seasoned investment writer. There is no shame in admitting that you need help and good advice when it comes to investing. If you owned an NBA basketball team, it would be in your best interest to hire a seasoned coach to guide and mentor your players. Same with investing, it is in your best interest to seek out the advice of a well-respected investment analyst/writer who can help you identify good investment opportunities that warrant your own further research and due diligence. An investment in knowledge reaps the best rewards, and that could not be more true when it comes to investment education, whether it be paying for access to pay-walled articles in an online open-source investment community such as Seeking Alpha or for access to an investment newsletter published by a well-respected author/analyst with a solid track record in publications such as Forbes and Morningstar. By the way, some brokers actually offer Morningstar research on individual stocks for free as a benefit for being their client.

An amateur investor may feel the bravado to go at analyzing investments alone, but like most people, he probably has a day job and family and friend commitments that takes up most of his time. Reading annual reports and analyzing companies from top to bottom one-by-one can be fun, but is immensely time consuming and is unrealistic for most people to do as an initial starting point. While you should still do research on your own, you should do it after you get help in identifying where the opportunities are in the first place. Advice from trusted experts significantly cuts down the amount of time it takes to identify good investment opportunities. In the end, by surrounding yourself with expert investment writers, you are saving not only valuable time but also avoiding pitfalls that you may not have identified on your own and that in itself is well-worth the cost of a monthly subscription.

Another reason to pay for advice is because studies show that you are more likely to utilize advice that you pay for. As the saying goes, "Free advice often goes ignored". Imagine if you got nutritional advice from a friend. You'll probably nod out of respect and forget about it on your way home. Why is that? The reason is two-fold. First, you probably don't entirely trust that your friend knows what he is talking about since he is not professionally trained in the study of nutrition. Second, since you did not trade a piece of your personal worth for this piece of advice, you are mentally conditioned to value it much less than if you had traded something for it.

Say instead you actually do the homework of seeking out a nutritional specialist and paid for their advice. You would probably not only remember what they tell you, but also write it down lest you forget it and apply it to your everyday living. That's because you have invested both your time and money in seeking a reputable person and have placed a value on the paid advice they are giving you. You have mentally conditioned yourself to be receptive to that advice and will be more likely to do further research and act on that advice.

I must add that simply paying for advice does not mean you will get quality or suitable advice for your investment needs. There are certainly some investment analysts out there that have questionable track records, and you would be better off going at it alone than following their advice. So how do you sift the good from the bad? Before following any author, I make sure to check out their past articles and recommendations and see how they panned out over time. This is especially easy to do in online investment communities. In addition, reading their past articles can give you a sense of their investment philosophy and whether it matches with yours. For example, if you are a conservative investor and want to seek out recession proof companies that can weather any economic cycle, then you should look for an analyst or advisory service such as Simply Safe Dividends that share in that same investment philosophy.

In addition, it is in your best interest as an investor to hear from all sides regarding a potential investment, in what is called the bull and bear theses. Hearing from all sides helps to sharpen your mental focus on the risk vs reward of a potential investment. There is no such thing as a perfect investment, so having a well-balanced understanding of the risk vs reward of any investment helps you to make an informed decision that minimizes your risk and maximizes your chances of success in any given investment opportunity.

Epilogue

I hope you enjoyed reading this book as much as I did writing it. My intent from day one of writing is to help readers understand that investing is not only about numbers and profits, but also about feeling engaged with the society in which we live. I strongly believe that this mindset, coupled with a value-minded approach can lead to outsized income and capital gains from your investments over the long term. I'm going to leave you with a few final nuggets of wisdom that I think summarizes points in this book and that have been guiding principles for me.

A good defense is better than a strong offense – Expert long term investors know that investing should be more about managing risk than trying to beat the market. A selection of well-run companies with durable businesses (more recession resistance) that pay a safe and growing dividend and purchased at value prices is better than hunting for the 'next best thing' that everyone is talking about (with a high share price to match).

The stock market is designed to transfer wealth from the active to the patient – Be patient with your holdings. Don't sell your holdings as long as the fundamental thesis for your original purchase is not broken. Do your due diligence and learn to take advantage of over-pessimism by purchasing shares of your favorite companies whenever they are mispriced.

Investing is as much an art as it is a science – All of the quantitative metrics and ratios in the world cannot help an investor make the right decisions without complementing them with proper qualitative judgement. Principles discussed in this book such as suitability, durability of cash flows, recession resilience, moats, and likelihood of technological disruption should all be factored in along with earnings growth, valuation, dividend payout, and debt metrics also discussed. Put your critical thinking hat on and think equally about what could go right versus what could go wrong.

Valuation Matters – Minimize risk to your portfolio by purchasing well-researched stocks that you like when the market is overly pessimistic about them. This builds an inherent margin of safety for you. Think of it as a market for stocks rather than the stock market, and there is always some stocks that are on sale even the stock market as a whole is overpriced.

Seek advice from others – No matter how great of a stock analyst you think you are, there is always room for getting new ideas to help with identifying opportunities and weaknesses that you may have missed, whether it be from online investment communities such as Seeking Alpha, or from analyst research reports such as Morningstar. You may not necessarily agree with the opinions of others and should always have a healthy level of skepticism, but giving consideration to different perspectives broadens your horizons and sharpens your skills as an investor.

Be picky about what you buy – You don't have to buy a company just because it is trading at a cheap price. Focusing on a 'forever hold' mentality will allow you to sharpen your focus and ask the tough questions and do the research before buying any stock. The more stocks you are willing to evaluate, the more wrong stocks you can filter out before finding the right ones for you.

A market for stocks rather than the stock market – You can find bargains in high-quality individual stocks even when the market index is trading at an all-time high. The key is to follow a wide range of stocks in a number of different industries. At any point in time, an industry or stock will fall out of favor due to overly negative sentiment and/or temporary headwinds, thereby causing the stock to be mispriced.

Diversification is key – There are no guarantees that any one investment will work out, but by being selective with your choices, and applying the criteria mentioned in this book, you can minimize your risk and maximize your chances for success.

Again, thank you for reading my book, and I wish you all the best in your investment journey.